CW01501521

Dedication

What **CAN** I Control? is dedicated to the
memory of my friends who died in the Royal
Marsden Cancer Hospital and to their loving families
who also consistently showed me love like I was
their own son.

Thank You, you're not forgotten

Contents

To Ivor,

WHAT
CAN
I CONTROL?

THE CRUCIAL LIFE LESSONS OF A 2X CANCER SURVIVOR

KIERRAN JARRETT

Thank you for Having
Me! Every obstacle is a chance
for you to be tested and for
your faith to be Tried. *Kierrajne*
Apply faith and overcome!

Copyright © 2017 by Kierran Jarrett
All rights reserved. Written permission must be
secured from the publisher to use or reproduce any
part of this book, except for brief quotations in
critical reviews or articles.
Publisher: KLJ Publishing House
Photography: Charles Sterling Photography
Distributed by: KLJ Publishing House
IBSN: 978-1977906458

WHAT **CAN** I CONTROL?
The crucial life lessons I learned whilst beating cancer TWICE!

Introduction

Ok, let's get a few things clear before we dive into the purpose of this book. I'm going to be very transparent throughout this book. Please believe that I am going to make you question yourself throughout the upcoming passages.

Not to talk down to you by any means, the idea is to explain to you that I understand your struggle. I myself have also had my weak points, however, the simple reality is there are things IN YOUR LIFE that you CAN control even if life throws things at you that you feel you can't and if you start to take charge of how you think, it can allow you to free yourself from a lot of the pressures that life chucks at us daily. At this moment, you're probably questioning my credibility to talk to you about anything. You don't know me and odds are we have never met, so what could I possibly teach you?

Well, Let me introduce myself.

My name is Kierran and I am a 24 year old Business Studies and Marketing graduate, who graduated from the University of Hertfordshire with a 2:1 and a Dean's Award.

So, why the book? Well, before my graduation, in 2015 at the age of 21 there wasn't much I could say to you regarding the struggles of life that we all didn't already know. Back then I was studying at University, and there weren't many worries at this time besides the obvious which was the fact that I had to pass my exams, which is a common struggle for many students.

However, in 2015 January while studying for my final year at University, I was diagnosed with cancer, Leukemia to be precise, (cancer of the blood) and the way in which it happened is a book in itself. However, if I were about to give you a short version of the story so that you are all caught up, I would start by explaining the fact that the diagnosis itself came out of nowhere. While I was at University, I managed to get bitten on my finger which caused my whole left hand to swell up.

After a period had passed (around two weeks), I began to realise that MY BODY simply wasn't fighting the infection. Typically, as a guy, we don't really get clinical check-ups, unless suddenly you are having second thoughts about your relationship with a certain individual *cough*, or in my case, I was forced to go by my mother who decided that it was time to go, even though I objected as I was busy at the time. Rather than make it a big thing, I went to the clinic, and the doctors took blood from me and began to run their tests. Within 48 hours I was diagnosed with cancer. It turns out I had Leukemia and based upon my blood work it looked like I had had it for a while. The scary thing was, they told me it was super lucky that they caught it when they did. They even went as far as to tell me (because I wasn't trying to do chemotherapy initially) that based on my blood work and how quickly the cancerous cells where duplicating, that if I didn't get treatment soon I could die in one week because I basically didn't have a functioning immune system. Hence why a bug bite had me walking around South East London with a swollen hand!

Considering the news put before me, I went through a lot emotionally and spiritually. I was angry at life, God and everything in between.

I then eventually decided to take the course of treatment provided and after seven months of chemotherapy, in August 2015 I was released with the 'All Clear' and I was declared to be in remission. You can imagine that I was very excited which lead to a celebratory surprise "You Beat Cancer Party" of sorts. It was a delightful surprise with friends & family and once that was over and I had some time to rest, it was back to University to finish my degree. It went well, very well actually…. For around four months.

Then, POW! as if it was planned, in January 2016 the following year on the same day as the previous year, after having my monthly blood check-up, it was confirmed that I had relapsed. For those who don't understand the severity of the situation, this means that the cancer cells were back and not only were they back, but they were stronger and now harder to kill. A wave of emotions hit me at once. I was crushed, devastated and emotional. Initially, I felt like I was going to throw up simply based on the news. I couldn't believe that after beating cancer, surviving after I was told I had one week to live, celebrating the fact and then going back to University, that I was about to do it all again!

So, what did I learn? It was the difference between my initial bout with cancer and my relapse that is the premise for this book. The first time I was diagnosed I simply reacted to the information that was given to me, as I will explain as you continue to read this book. However, my initial encounter with the disease prepared me for my second encounter and the way in which I chose to fight it.

The ultimate lesson which I want to share in this book is the fact that you CAN control situations if you focus on controlling how you react to them.

Chapter 1: Deal With It

Probably not the best name for a chapter that is designed to motivate you, but it is a crucial thing for you to consider which is why it comes first. The biggest lesson I learned and that I need you to understand is that there is always something that YOU CAN control! For example, I could not control getting cancer the first time or the second time. What I could control is the way in which I reacted to the situation presented to me. In other words, I could control how I dealt with it. The ability to take back some control from the battering of life is what helped me deal with cancer… the second time.

Why only the second time? Well, I didn't take the news too well the first time, as we will talk about in this book. My most humbling moments and lessons came because of my initial encounter with cancer. Then the Universe decided to test if I really learned anything at all and I was given a chance to apply it through my second encounter with the disease. I'm not going to sit here and act like I'm happy that I was diagnosed twice, but I'm grateful for what I learned. Learning that we all have the power to control things in our space and in our lives directly, was not something I had even previously contemplated during my first battle with cancer. In fact, it was quite the opposite. I literally went through the motions of feeling sorry for myself, complaining, fighting and arguing with loved ones and also with doctors. Many arguments stemmed from disagreements about what they were telling me I needed to do for treatment as opposed to what I wanted to do. I even told Christian Leaders and nurses about themselves all the while getting frustrated, asking "why me?" The truth is I was reacting to the news, plain and simple.

Let us imagine for a second that you're in a fight OK? Now imagine yourself on the defensive, your opponent is throwing punches continuously so much so that you can't even go on the offensive. All you can do is duck, weave, and block. Believe it or not, that's how many of our lives are lived! Some are fighting emotions such as depression, anxiety or loss, others with negative energies and negative people who for some could be their managers at the job or even family.

Simply put, life for many people has yet to be "LIVED."

The second time I was diagnosed this was not the case. My initial thought was understandably emotional. However, the one great thing about taking a Loss or an "L" in this life is that as long as you're breathing you can learn from your life experiences and try again. Relapsing is where I had to look at my situation and seriously rethink. How did the last time work out when I had the opportunity to control my emotions? The truth is not too well! Even today, months after I have been given the all clear, my friends still tell me of the way in which I spoke to them when I was diagnosed. Supposedly they thought that we weren't friends any more. I personally don't remember this however, because I do know that I was incredibly angry during my first year, as I hadn't fully dealt with my emotions in my current reality, so I haven't questioned it. As far as control goes, from the very beginning, I was very aware of the power of the mind and also the "Law of Attraction" as talked about by Napoleon Hill. Let me ask you this. Have you ever been presented with a problem that you overcame because you dug deep or found a part of you that was overly willing to fight the situation at hand? Think carefully for a second. It could be exams, relationships, money or even at your workplace. I believe that there is a fighter in all of us that is entirely capable of dealing with the onslaught of life and can shift our thinking at the same time.

One thing I found out when going through my own struggle is that it's down to mindset and the way you chose to look at life. The choice is important and I believe perception is key. Perception is defined in the dictionary as "the way in which something is regarded, understood, or interpreted." I believe that what one man sees as life attacking him, another man sees as an opening to attack a problem. If you have ever seen a boxing match or studied some fighting, you'll see that it's essential to use someone's strength against them. A lot of martial arts are built on this principle. Believe it or not, you must understand that life means you no harm and at the same time it doesn't care about you. The Universe doesn't see your colour, your height or gender etc. Its sole purpose is to pressure you till you wake up and become smarter, stronger and wiser.

Often the smartest people in this world, the richest people in this world, the most looked up to people in this world are people who took the cards life handed them, took the blows it gave them and then overcame the odds to do incredible things. From Gandhi to Nelson Mandela to Dr. Martin Luther King, to Alan Sugar to Jay Z. These are the people that the world wants to hear speak, these are people that people idolise and look up to. Why? Because life attacks us all! The question I want you to ask yourself when you're next approached with a dilemma is when all is said and done, HOW DID YOU DEAL WITH IT?

The elephant in the room that I want to deal with in this first initial chapter is that, contrary to the title of this book there are some things in life that you simply CAN'T CONTROL! For example, cancer, however what you can control is how you deal with it based upon your outlook and perception. The controlling of your reactive emotions is just as important as the situation you are now dealing with. As this book continues, you will see that I talk about a range of emotions, as I intend to show you openly and honestly what I learned and continued to learn about control of my life and my journey through my two years of battling cancer.

Chapter 2: Who Will Love Me?

I was never really worried about love before being ill. Like most people, there is somewhat of an expectation that life will present opportunities for you to find love and when it comes around, it is then your choice to decide if you are ready to receive it or wait for another opportunity. With that in mind, one thing I had never experienced growing up was a lack of worth, until I was diagnosed with cancer. The disease itself wasn't really that much of an issue compared to the thoughts that plagued my mind regarding treatment. As a young man in his twenties with the hope of being a father one day, for doctors to be telling me that the treatment will lessen my ability to have kids, was devastating and hurt me more than the treatment ever could. Based upon this shocking information, the mind started asking questions, questions and hypotheticals that I myself couldn't answer and was also fearful of. Questions like, who will love me if this procedure damages me to the extent that I can't have kids? Wouldn't that make me a broken man? Half a man? Maybe I shouldn't tell anyone that I date about the effects of treatment till after we're married. I was literally going through it. I have never struggled with my self-image to this extent, which then ultimately lead to self-loathing. I started to believe that I wasn't capable of being loved. Don't get me wrong, God's love and family love are great, but they are in a completely different category to the love received by a spouse or partner. The thought of never having this sent me into a depression and negative thought cycle.

Contrary to the last chapter, I genuinely didn't know how to deal with this one and so I had to look for external help. The biggest piece of advice I got wasn't from preachers or my parents but my Ex girlfriend. Right!? So all of you who are burning bridges with your exs…. *cough* … never mind let's keep it moving. I ended up traveling to south London to basically confine in her and to vent. The great thing about not breaking up badly from intimate relationships is that at one point this person loved you or had some higher form of love outside of friendship and because of this will genuinely lift you up in your dark moments. My Ex who we will call Jen is a talented singer with quite a dull character who generally tends to get straight to the point. This may sound harsh and don't get me wrong we have had our disputes, but her heart-warming vibe and mannerisms are something that you genuinely feel and reciprocate when she speaks. I am a firm believer that the heart in which someone advises you is key to recognising a person's intent.

As I poured out my concerns the first thing she suggested was "Let's go for a walk, " and as we did so, I began to state everything that I had previously reported. She listened at first and then said the most profound thing. She said, "You're thinking like a man, you're way too logical", which was then followed by, "Women love differently to men, we can love you throughout your ups and downs because our love is different. A woman who loves you for you will decide to do so knowing who you are and with your flaws. The worst thing you could do is lie initially because the wrong woman will love you based upon the options you have stated, and when you later reveal the real you, she may end up not liking you because you're not what she signed up for. HOWEVER, there will be a woman who loves you for you regardless, if you're honest from the get go." Now if I'm 100% honest, I wasn't trying to hear this. You've probably guessed that I fought her on this like I fight everyone else. She later explained that this is something I need to own and that her faith in God gave her the will to believe that everything will be ok concerning me. As you may have guessed like anyone else who has ever been through anything tough or challenging, you're thinking to yourself "It is easy for you to be positive, you're not in my situation." However, I left it there, and we prayed and departed ways. I was uplifted at the moment, but in reality, I wasn't convinced. So, I asked myself, what can I control? and in this case, the answer was absolutely nothing LOL which is the sad truth. All I could do is pray and hope that God heard me. In some way, I think God or the Universe, (whatever you call your spiritual higher power) heard me. The answer didn't come for a while, in fact, it came the next year during my relapse year.

During May, just before my bone marrow transplant in June, it was time for me to take my 3rd year University exams. I actually had no idea where I was going to stay as I lived really far from my University, and it was a full week of exams. A lot of people I called friends actually rejected the premise of me staying with them. Something to do with concentrating on exams and the fact they didn't want me to be a distraction. Looking back on it we can all recognise that this was an excuse, especially considering the circumstances, but they thought what they thought, and there wasn't much I could do. I was getting stressed. I didn't do a whole year's worth of coursework in a hospital while juggling chemotherapy not to be able to take the exam! Luckily one of the friends finally accepted my request, and she let me stay at her house, which was full of females who were studying to be radiographers/ nurses. Ironic, right? and as God would have it, the next week I was blessed to stay with a girl who we will call Lin.

This amazing lady was the only person who was currently still at University willing accommodated me. Listen. This girl took care of me the entire week I stayed over. Fed me, made me feel at home, looked after me, studied with me, made me go to the library, chilled with me and even prayed with me. This is one of those times God blesses you and you truly know that God answers prayers. I LANDED ON MY FEET.. LOL and I thank God every day because without this person I would never have been able to take my exams and graduate with a 2:1 whilst knowing that the week after I would need to go in for radiotherapy and a bone marrow transplant. So, why bring her up you say? Well as time went on we became close and she confirmed the words that Jen had stated the year before. Lin let me know that she liked me for who I was and was fully open to the idea of us dating and even potentially being serious, with someone like me even knowing my problems.

I was blown away; gobsmacked actually. A year ago, I was getting upset to the point of feeling ill, questioning will anyone love me, the year later God presents someone to me, who truly does. We did not end up dating in the end, however. The reason was simple; my main focus was surviving the treatment and getting healthy. I didn't feel right now was the time to take on the emotional pressure of dating, and so we put the idea on pause.

Jen and Lin! These two women blessed me incredibly and therefore had to be mentioned. There are situations that life will throw at you that you CAN NOT control. With that being understood, the love of others can provide a perspective that you would have never contemplated and should be seriously taken into consideration and accepted. The biggest lesson learned from this whole experience (as far as love goes) is that the mind is a great tool and allows a person to accomplish some incredible feats, but it is also an enemy of itself. I conjured up thoughts that did not match my reality. The same mind that was trying to keep my spirits lifted was the same mind trying to tear me down. So again, I guess the question is still…

WHAT CAN I CONTROL? In this scenario, the ability to control one's imaginative thoughts is the key. I conjured a reality in my mind that didn't match the real world. This led me to feel a certain way, which then started to shape my reality. Had it not been for the women in my life, that may still potentially be the case, which could have led to a closed minded view, which inevitably would have left me alone and bitter at life.

Chapter 3: Positive Thinking

Yup! You guessed it. Please don't skip this chapter. I know it's tempting, but let's face it, this is a very important topic. Many people only apply positive thinking when it comes to specific goals, like a promotion at work or for their sports team to succeed, but what about when it's pouring with rain outside? Can you still activate positive thinking then? The reality is, if it were sunny you'd be a lot more confident in your ability to look me in the face and say "Yes, I'd be positive" however, in this scenario given it's raining and no one is really trying to go battle with the forces of nature, are you still positive?

Ok, so what is positive thinking? Is it lying to yourself? Telling yourself everything will be ok even when life is clearly showing you a roadmap to disaster? Some call this faith, and some call it denial. No matter what your belief is, we can all agree there is a power in us to see a negative reality and perceiver through it using our ability to think different. Remember what I said about perception?

Positive thinking is the ability to see a stumbling block as a footstool. It has nothing to do with faith or denial. Positive thinking is choosing to see what's in front of you and making it work in your favour. A perfect example would be the book you are currently reading. Before me having cancer, I had absolutely no intention to write any type of book about anything. Not only that, I didn't have anything to say or to share. The voice/ platform that I now have comes from the negative process of surviving a battle, which many people did not survive, Twice!

Let me ask you a serious question. What battle are you fighting? Is it a battle that you think you're losing? Or is it a chance for you to show the warrior that you are? In the art of war, a battle is a perfect time to look for a promotion. The more opponents you kill and also the way in which you defend your brothers and sisters on the field of battle, contribute to the likelihood of you being recognised when the battle was over.

Thinking differently, acting differently, speaking differently. These are all choices and choices you can make daily, moving you towards a more positive end.

When I was first diagnosed with cancer, I was very negative. The pressure of being ill, dropping out of University, the continuous thoughts of not being loved, being in pain and looking at my body as it began to change, as I went through chemo. Positive thinking saved me from myself; it saved my life. From my own experience, there is nothing wrong with drawing on the positivity of other people. When I was in the hospital, I had many visits from friends and family, some of which I hadn't seen in years who simply wanted to come and show support. Let us not kid ourselves; there will be days when your positivity tank is empty. You're human, and this is part of life. However, before you go for the ice cream and your favourite slow song, make sure that you surround yourself with people who will lift you up.

There were days; sometimes weeks when I didn't even look at my phone or social media. I was that down! I told all my friends and family not to visit me, as I was feeling that low. I wasn't feeling positive and I was comfortable being miserable. Lucky for me, my family (mostly my aunties) are hard of hearing and they visited me even when I said don't. In their visits, they poured out their love for me and their hope for my wellbeing even though I thought that I didn't want it. As a result, it helped me recover out of my slump. I say all that to say this; I'm not saying don't eat the ice cream, I'm simply advising that if you're going to eat it, that you eat it WITH someone and with someone who will keep you in positive spirits.

Finally, I feel it's important to give you a real example of how positive thinking saved my life. The cancer ward I happened to be in was called the Teenage Cancer Ward and was located at the Royal Marsden Hospital. Due to the support of different charities and the fact that Prince William is the President of the hospital, following in his mother's footsteps, Princess Diana, the ward was brand new. There were PlayStations, snooker tables, HD TVs, colourful rooms and the ward had above average hospital food. Besides treatment itself, we as patients really didn't have much to complain about and so the basic vibe from the patients was positive and enjoyable because we would muck about, talk about things we saw on social media and play games.

The more time you spent the in hospital, the more people you came across and therefore now and then a new patient would be admitted. Normally we (the patients who had been there for a while) would try our best to welcome them, and everything would go smoothly, therefore, adding to the generic positive energy of the ward. However, there is also a different type of patient that would occasionally get admitted. The patient that would come and be SOOOOO depressing. Now granted everyone handles being diagnosed with cancer differently. Please understand this isn't a comparison between people, but more of an observation. Those that came into the hospital with that type of energy always struggled the most with their treatment and in some cases, it even resulted in death.

The reality of controlling how you think is that it's not just so you can be happy 24/7 (which again, is not realistic) but it's healthy. It's good for your mind, for your perception of life and your relationships and friendships.

There is nothing wrong with sourcing positivity from outside sources. I gained a lot of positivity from people such as comedians @MikesComdey, @ReggieCouz, @HAHAdavis// @_Cornell__ // @Young_ezee_etc but also from people I had worked with before my illness.

There was a man I used to work with, we still talk now actually, but back then we were business partners. He was my age, but he was a lot taller than me. He always carried himself like he was older than me and his name was Jerome Lancaster. Now Lancaster, gave me two critical talks in my life, one when I was initially diagnosed and one when I was diagnosed the second time.

He also is a Christian, consistently shared his love for God that allowed him to believe that I would be ok. Not only that, he constantly checked up on me too even though he ran his own business, which took a great deal of time.

In one of these encounters, we sat in Westfield shopping mall, and he only asked "Are you scared?" now, believe it or not, this isn't a question I was asked a lot. In fact, it's almost like everyone else purposely didn't ask me that question as they must have thought I would get worried or something. At which point I basically poured out all the negativity I had been holding and basically regurgitated everything that was going on in my head to which he replied "This isn't going to kill you, I actually don't see you dying, not because I'm your friend or anything, but simply based on the fact, my belief in your will to live, stops me from worrying about you. Therefore I know that Gods got you, you'll be fine man."

In other words, he knew no matter what, that there was never going to be any point where he was truly going to hear me say anything too negative that ventured anything close to giving up and therefore this then gave him the faith to in turn give me faith. I believe even when faced with a situation that warrants fear, you can still choose to be positive. He was so positive that he even put on a boxing event, to raise money for the supporting charity that was helping me through treatment.

Here's how being positive can bless those around you. Before my first year fighting cancer, I had been attending University for two years. Whist attending, I was lucky enough to be able to befriend a group of guys that I still keep in contact with even today. Amarni, Callumn, Taiwo, and Victor and they consistently helped me out with small things throughout my time studying. HERE is WHY I mention them.

There is something to be said when people are consistent with who they are, as individuals even in the worst times. One of my most memorable experiences during my first year of treatment was being in a bay in the Teenage Cancer Ward, surrounded by curtains and hearing "Yo G, My n****, Where this Guy at!" LOL. They damn near scared the rest of the patients! Even when they saw me, they didn't change their energy. We played FIFA, and they spoke to me, and each other just like how we used to talk when we were at University. This blessed me more than you'll ever know because they were one of the few initial groups of people to see me and they never gave an ounce of negative vibes towards me, even whilst lying in the hospital bed.

My own twin brother Pearce who would see me nearly every day after work and my school friends were the same. They came and saw me also and started making jokes right from the moment they saw me. One of the guys by the name of Sam saw me and straight away he said "You look way too healthy at this current moment for me to feel sorry for you (my hair had not yet fallen out), so you aren't getting any of that from me" and from there he, like the rest of my friends treated me normally and really hid all signs of concern and sadness, which is exactly what I wanted and needed. Their happiness and smiles brought me joy. It was like everyone who visited me who was my age had faith in my survival before I did and therefore refused to be negative in any way.

As I have lived through this experience on a personal level, I practice being positive daily, even via social media. I used to write statuses and indirect remarks all over the place like a mad man, however nowadays I thrive more of positivity than having people worry about me. With this being said, not everyone will be positive for you, or at least not in a way where you will be willing to receive it. Some people need to be given space so that you can indeed keep your energy positive.

Chapter 4: Limited Association During Times of Process

I am acutely aware that I said to be positive and I'm not backtracking, I promise. However, as one of my brothers by the name of 'Virgo' told me, "burn the bridge dude, I'll even buy you the matches!" What was he talking about? He was directly insinuating that there are some people you generally can't keep around. At least not for now anyway or maybe just in small doses. People that encourage you to build you up, correct you in love, want to see you win, want to see you happy, want the very best for you – keep them around, add foundations to those relationships, build experiences with those people and reciprocate the love.

There is another type of person. The one where after you finish talking to them you feel a weight lifted off your shoulders. The type of person where you see their name come up on your phone and you sigh before you even pick up. The person you slowly feel yourself naturally distancing from because they are emotionally draining.

Virgo would call these people vultures, but since vultures only tend to go for dead animals (and I'm hoping your dreams and aspirations are very much alive) let's call these people "leeches." Now here's the thing. Leeches are not evil. They simply run on instinct. No person truly wants to be dependent on another person, and yet life can knock people back in such a way they can feel the need to be cynical and life draining as a means of survival. Depending on how close you are to these people that cause you to feel this way, will also determine to what degree you lessen your association or energy towards them. If they are an acquaintance, then a quick chop will probably need to happen. However, if they are more than that then what do you do?

Holton Buggs who is an IBO (Independent Business Owner) For Organo Gold, in 2016 was earning a whopping $1,150,000 a month and he said this:

"I have a limited association. What is this you ask? I have people in my life that knew me before I was a millionaire. To them, I'm not a millionaire I'm simply Holton Buggs, and it's great because they treat me like I'm a normal person. However, I don't hang with these people. This has nothing to with them personally, but for me to be great, I need to consistently be around people who think like me or better, that's the only way to be successful in anything."

So, why am I mentioning this? Well, I'm not one to truly cut people off, at least not for a long amount of time, especially not family. Nevertheless, in the hospital, I had to "limit" certain family from visiting me. Now, I'm not about in any way shape or form to call any of my own family "leeches" or "vultures" but just follow me on this. Let's take my mother (yes, I'm going to be very careful with what I'm about to say, I'm more than sure she will read this book at some point). My mum loves me, and I love her. My mum, although we have never always seen eye to eye, has been a consistent source of kindness, wisdom, and hope in my life from a young child into my adult life. Like most mums, my mum did what most mothers do and she "loved" through my troubling experience. Almost too much. I had to stop (more like a BAN) my own mother from seeing me in the hospital, and the reason for this was because her love for me and the way in which she loved sometimes came across negatively because every time I would cough or shake a little or even itch! A simple itch! She would try and call the nurse or ask if I was ok. Now the first few times, it was comforting, the 4th or 5th time its borderline annoying however the 10th time in the space of 20 minutes…. I then decided it's time for you to go home mum, GO…HOME lol.

I say this to prove a point to you. Some people mean you nothing but love. It wasn't just family; it was friends too. If any of my friends visited me and consistently felt sorry for me, I'd also tell them "start smiling, it's ok, if you can't see me in this state and stay positive then Whatsapp me because I can't have you in this space, with my mindset focused on fighting this."

(Disclaimer: Do not confuse what I am saying about burning bridges for the sake of your vision and purpose and energy with not being able to take constructive criticism and correction from those that know better because I will throw you under the bus if you bring me or this book up in your defence. There is a strict difference LOL)

The point I'm making is simple. This is something you can definitely control. In this instance, cutting people off is fully within your capability and it is fully within your rights. This isn't something you need to feel bad about doing either. Some people just don't mix, or can't mix all the time, and that's just life. Controlling whose around you and when they are around you can be crucial to many decisions you make in this life. Who is comforting you? And sharing their optimism? On the other hand, who's pessimistic and negative? Control it! Burn the bridge, if you care for them, when you reach your desired goal, by all means, bring them back into your life however, if this is not the case, I suggest you walk away.

I can fully appreciate you may not necessarily want to cut anyone off in the short term, maybe due to a fear of loss? But in the long term, you'll notice the difference to your mindset and your well-being and all in all your day-to-day happiness.

Chapter 5: Dealing With Loss

The loss in its entirety is painful.

Why? Well, because most things that are considered losses are things that were once a part of your daily routine, something that you may have become accustomed to or maybe something which has always been and you never contemplated life without. Until it's gone.

I had never experienced true loss before my battle with Leukaemia. I mean, we have all lost material things growing up, a wallet or a pair of headphones, which then meant that we would have to deal with the absence of said item for a while. No matter how angry it makes us, the majority of us find ourselves not being able to overreact too much because internally we know that "we can always get another one." Which is normal and rational when you think about it. Why cry over something you can proactively fix yourself? The issue is, life doesn't have that "Try again" button when it comes to your existence. The breath in your lungs, the thoughts in your mind, the smile on your face or even the love in your heart. Life is one of the few things you only get one chance at doing and when it is your time to go, you're gone. Forever etched into the tapestry of the lives you have been able to touch while still present.

Again, I can only speak for myself. Prior to having cancer, I have never felt true loss. No immediate family members had passed and I never knew my Grandparents on my mum's side or at least not at an age where I had a real memory, meanwhile all other family members are alive and kicking. However, being in a cancer ward, you almost get used to death (not because people are dying every day, God Forbid!) but simply because you know that its a reality that is now imposing itself on your space and you can't ignore it.

Now during my time in hospital there were a few of us that became quite close. Luckily, I was blessed enough to be in the teenage cancer ward so everyone was pretty much in my age bracket. There were two wards, a male and a female and so I really didn't get to develop much of a relationship with the female patients except for the occasional passing waves and smiles as you journeyed passed their bay to go to see the nurses or go to the kitchen. As for the lads in my ward, there was myself, Matt, Eshant, Monir, Andy, and Alex. Now there were actually a lot more people who I crossed paths with from

Brighton to Gibraltar, however for the sake of my point lets chop it down to these five individuals.

The reason I've chosen these five is that I personally spent the most time with these people, either in a group or on a one on one basis. From betting packets of Oreos on FIFA matches to opening the other person's blinds early the next morning (because you lost said match) and going back to bed like you did nothing.

As lively as it seems, please do not forget, we all had cancer. Granted they varied, from tumours to leukaemia to other blood diseases…… and this is where it gets real.

These people had been there for me; I had been there for them. We had seen each other suffer, we would check up on each other, ask nurses about each other, share experiences and advice with each other. When our families had gone home, these people were the ones annoying you, laughing with you, watching TV with you basically we became a hospital family, with the nurses as our parents. But then…

One day, not long after being cancer free the first time around in 2015, I came in for a routine monthly check-up and it just so happened that Monir was there too. Now Monir was a young Moroccan guy and he wanted to study mechanics and engineering at college and University. Most times he had on a serious face and posture, but as soon as you said hi to the guy, his face would change, and he would be all smiles. I sat next to him, and we caught up, asked each other about our wellbeing, laughed and joked till our names were called to see our individual Consultants. He was called. First, we hugged it out, and he went to see his Consultant.

Not long after that he came out, pale as a ghost, his mum followed behind him holding back tears. Honestly, I had never seen him or his mum like that before. From what I remember, that was the moment when they told him that the treatment wasn't working. I tried to ask what happened, but mixed with anger and shock, he said to me "I need more treatment."

Monir had been waiting for a transplant for a little bit, just like me, and even though his sister was a match, he needed to be in remission before the hospital would do that transplant, but the cancer would not go into remission. Naturally, in my head, I'm thinking, "it's sad, but he's a fighter, he'll be ok, ill check up on him weekly to keep him company."

Within a week, he Died… I found out two weeks later from his sister. In his culture, it is the custom that they bury the body within 48 hours of death…… I NEVER got to say goodbye; I never got to say thanks, I never got to encourage or even go to the funeral. This was my first encounter with death, on a personal level.

Coming from a Christian background, we have a prayer that we say in times of trouble:

Security of the One Who Trusts in the LORD from Psalms 91:

He who ⁽ᵃ⁾ dwells in the shelter of the Most High
Will remain secure and rest in the shadow of the Almighty [whose
power no enemy can withstand].

2

I will say of the LORD, "He is my refuge and my fortress,
My God, in whom I trust [with great confidence, and on whom I
rely]!"

3

For He will save you from the trap of the fowler,
And from the deadly pestilence.

4

He will cover you and completely protect you with His pinions,
And under His wings you will find refuge;
His faithfulness is a shield and a wall.

5

You will not be afraid of the terror of night,
Nor of the arrow that flies by day,

6

Nor of the pestilence that stalks in darkness,

Nor of the destruction (sudden death) that lays waste at noon.
7

A thousand may fall at your side
And ten thousand at your right hand,
But danger will not come near you.

It's a very common Psalm. This prayer was said so many times by my family and friends and was very encouraging at times. However, it lost its appeal when Monir died. Reread v7 in the BOLD writing. I'll wait……

Please understand, I'm super glad to be alive, I truly am. I am also aware that this Psalm was written by King David who was a warrior, so the analogy makes perfect sense in context. However, what the prayer didn't do for me, was comfort me when in reality people were really dying, on my right hand and by my side and now the prayer no longer seemed like a blessing. I actually didn't know how much it bothered me till the following year January 2016.

January 2016! The month I was diagnosed with cancer for the SECOND TIME and straight away, all the buried emotions about Monir poured to the surface. I was in the same room that he was in when they told him there was nothing that they could do for him, so naturally, my mind wandered down the same path.

During that year is when I met Alex. Andy also relapsed and was sent back to the hospital that year, so I had someone I could talk to, which did help a great deal. Alex was new to the ward, he had a brain tumour, but again he was one of the most positive people you could ever meet. Forever talking about "Jah" and becoming a farmer. I'm dead serious, this isn't a lie (lol) this whole battle made him re-evaluate his life in such a way, he was content with becoming a farmer. Unfortunately, both Andy and Alex both passed away that year as well.

Thankfully, I was well enough to go to their funerals and get some closure. Or so I thought... I continued to be troubled by my friend's deaths, I then realised I was dealing with survivor's guilt. Why am I alive? Why did they die? Now what? It's one thing to battle with survivor's guilt when it is just you and your emotions, it's another thing when you're at church one week, thanking God for your life, the next you're in a different church walking passed the crying parents of your friends who are lifeless in a casket. I struggled for a while to find a lesson in all this loss. To some degree, the lessons are still being learned, as I continue to live. One thing I will say is that you never know when people will go. Yes, we all got worries, bills, emotions, etc. but behind all of that make sure that you take the time to show those particular people in your life who are true blessings to you, how much you care about them, what they mean to you. Don't just say it, but show it and live your life aware of those that are supporting you. Personally, I have never been as aware of the importance of building better friendships and relationships as much as I am now. From my experience, I believe that friendships are something that you can consciously affect daily, making them stronger and more relevant. Build them daily.

Chapter 6: Not Once But Twice

A lot of people are amazed that I beat cancer twice. As a survivor, I really never understood their shock. My initial reasoning is because when you are given a sentence such as cancer, you basically have two options. Fight or let it happen. Anyone who has something to live for will probably choose to do the former if given the option. I guess, for this testimony to mean something I should probably explain my initial thought process from the first time I was diagnosed. Absolute disbelief …. The END!

No, but seriously lol I genuinely thought I was dreaming. I was in a cold, dusty hospital room in Lewisham with a busted bed and a needle in my arm being told I had cancer. 24/48 hours ago I was at work, going to meetings as a public motivational speaker on behalf of my network marketing company, to then be told that " Listen you could die if we don't go forward with treatment right away." So, as I said previously: ABSOLUTE DISBELIEF!

Remember what I said in the last chapter about not knowing when people may disappear? It was almost like every decision I had ever made came flooding back. People I didn't speak to, people I wish I spoke to more. People that I wanted to build with and spoke to about the future and now it seemed that my own light was about to be snuffed out.

I went through a range of emotions in the beginning, from fear to anger, to helplessness, to denial and even regret. Not to mention sadness, depression, and anxiety.

Oh? You thought this book was all going to be all "I knew from the beginning I had to think different...." NOPE. In fact, the lessons that I'm now sharing with you came as a by-product of the negative emotions that stirred within myself and the experiences that followed.

When all had been said and done, one of the main emotions left was anger. Mostly at God in all honesty. As someone raised in a faith-based household, I couldn't help but feel some resentment towards God. Was this his will? Why me and not the fat guy walking outside with gravy stains on his shirt? The worst part was also the fact that most of the people I was surrounded by were older people and all religious. Due to their faith (I'm not condemning anyone) they tended to use the same "bars" or "script" when consoling people. Tell me if you have ever heard any of these before, don't worry I'm pretty sure they are universal.

"God gives the hardest battles to his strongest fighters."

"God's got a plan, don't worry about it, you'll be fine."

And the famous *"It's a Test"* followed by some type of biblical reassurance. Now reading these phrases, you're probably thinking to yourself "I really don't see the problem here, these all sound really encouraging" and yes, you're correct, if it were a Sunday service I'd be thinking the same thing. Please remember though; I do not hear this from a place of calmness and neutrality, I hear all of this whilst engulfed in a spirit of anger. Every time God got brought up I would just get irritated, like someone who did me wrong just walked in the room like everything was ok.

For the sake of transparency ill share this with you:

For those that are not religious just try to follow for a second. Pre-treatment I was really struggling with my faith because of my diagnosis, because of this many people came to the house to wish me the best and to pray for me. Now please remember I'm still trying to process the fact that I could die and the fact that the hospital has issued a document that stated that I have one week to live. (No seriously, they issued a document saying that they expected me to crash physically because I didn't take chemotherapy when they told me to. Very cheeky, right?) so needless to say at this moment I am angry and I'm bitter at everyone. Anyway, so one of my mum's friends who is a Pastor, her mum who is also is a very spiritual woman plus a few other Christian individuals came to my house at the same time to pray for me. Again, they were super positive (with good intentions no doubt) which really aggravated me especially when they brought up God. I eventually snapped and quoted scripture to them all.

"Does not the bible say, 'If any of you come together in anything concerning me then I shall be in the midst?'… oh? …Does it? Great! Let us all pray RIGHT NOW, and I am going to try my hardest to believe and have faith, etc. and according to scripture! I should be healed…Correct? Because I honestly don't believe that it was God's will for me to die so young, OK So let's begin."

I'm not kidding; I actually said this and I wasn't joking either. So, everyone prayed, and I looked down at my infected hands, and I sighed and walked out the room and left them all in there.

I was hurt, I felt like God had left me, that the universe did a lucky dip, and my ticket has now been called, and it was my time to go, and that these people who had good intentions, at the end of the day really didn't understand what I was feeling or thinking.

Breathes in

Why am I saying all of this? The reality is simple. This all happened the first time I was diagnosed. As explained in this book already, a lot happened in my first year, I met people on the ward, people died, I had meaningful conversations with ex's and friends and with God that altogether had basically got me to a place emotionally where I had overcome the sickness in emotion and faith, before getting the all clear. The evidence of this came the following year when I was diagnosed a second time with a more aggressive form of leukaemia, which ultimately led me to have a bone marrow transplant with the help of "Anthony Nolan."

What had changed besides seven months of chemotherapy? Well by this point, all the emotions I was willing to give to this disease had already been used up. I was becoming too lazy to even acknowledge its power in my life, especially since I had already beat it. Secondly, what would I gain from going through the whole negative emotional rollercoaster again a second time?

I don't feel that anything bad comes from God, I do believe that there is an evil one that simply wants to do damage and harm to all, I therefore, believe it's by grace that we all get to function and act the way that we do as a people. With that being said (it's going to sound weird, especially considering how I was cussing initially my first year) when I was diagnosed the second time, I immediately thought "Ok, Game time."

Wait…
Hold on…
Don't roll your eyes….just wait…. Listen to me!
Let me explain… LOL

You can speak to anyone, my first year of treatment; I walked through it. Yes, I lost my hair, Yes I was sick a few times, and yes I nearly died twice. However, I cannot honestly tell you that in my first year ANY LESSONS were learned. Here is why. Firstly, I was in denial. I basically tried to act like me having cancer wasn't a reality. Secondly, I hadn't grown spiritually or emotionally during that seven-month period, and I was still overly PISSED at God. I even said and I quote "Nah, I'm sorry preacher, God won't get the glory out of this, Science will" and I said it with no hate and no malice, I just wasn't in a place to have any type of faith in God, as I didn't find what I was going through fair by any means. Remember what I said about no bad thing coming from God? I stick by it. However, that's not to say that part of me (even today) believes that God, saw my stubbornness and only took a step back and was like "Ok Kierran, ok" - "Devil, no lessons were learned, do what you want to do, let's see if he learns from this or is he just going to talk himself to death." For some reason, this whole idea isn't farfetched to me. In fact, the moment I was diagnosed a second time, I told the Consultant that I was not starting treatment. I know, right?! Instead for January, I fasted and prayed for the entire month of January with one of my best friends by the name of Yatta. THEN and only then did I feel prepared enough to take on the treatment. At which point I then felt emotionally "OK, Game on" See?! Makes more sense right? Sheesh..

Lessons can be learned from every life experience. For me, getting diagnosed a second time, taught me that there will always be some things in life that you CAN NOT control and yet the Universe, God, your inner spirit, (whatever you call the fighter in you, that makes you see a giant and instead of running away causes you start picking up stones with a smile on your face) whatever name you give it, will always provide an opportunity for you to face a problem with the correct mindset, if you choose to do so. If I'm honest I had one of the worst experiences of my cancer journey during my second diagnosis and yet the whole time, I was positive, I was emotionally stable, I had my faith back, I wasn't scared or nervous about my life and even though it was the worst few months of my life to date, I still managed to study in hospital and graduate from University with a 2:1.

The secret is simple; there is nothing new under the sun, every lesson you need to learn has already been learned by someone else. Once you source that knowledge, stand in the power of understanding and the company of like-minded people and you will look at problems and situations differently and use them as ways to make your faith stronger, rather than letting your faith be tested. In my case, my knowledge was that people had survived cancer before, and now I was also one of those people. I stood with people who believed that I would be ok, and prayed with me and for me thus keeping me in high spirits. This allowed me to attack the news differently to the first time I was diagnosed.

Chapter 7: Natural Vs. Medicine

I was actually asked to write about this because a lot of people who have gotten ill with cancer or who know someone with cancer always immediately tell you not to do the scientific route with chemotherapy and to undertake the herbalist route instead. Here is my experience with the two.

Initially, when I was first diagnosed in 2015, we didn't go ahead with medical treatment. A lot of family members started to try and put me off it. Telling me about "so & so" who died doing it or how bad it is and even that I should take to smoking marijuana or at least getting cannabis oil. Within days, the news of me getting cancer spread and my phone was full of messages, YouTube videos, and notifications on natural herbal remedies, which all sounded good, sometimes too good. However, it did open my eyes to that side of the medicinal spectrum. Personally, I don't trust a lot of things I see on the Internet, why? Because it's the Internet lol, so instead, what I decided to do is talk to a real-life herbalist who I was referred to by a family friend. The issue is, herbalists hate medical science, and scientists think herbalist are hippies who have very little evidence to back up their supernatural claims, whereas they have studies and trial. Both professions hate each other, and I didn't really know this until I went in for my first Consultation. I don't remember exactly what was said, as it was two years ago and he was using a bunch of words I had never heard before however, I did learn some interesting things. What I do remember is this. Herbal medicine has actually cured thousands of diseases across the globe, and the reason for this is simple. Everything man needed to make himself better he got from the ground before western medicine existed and the world span perfectly fine, and people lived long and prosperous lives. Which then begs the question? What is the need for western medicine?

Western medicine, in its raw form, is the copying of natural principles, manufactured for the masses, but the origin is the same. Personally, I believe that there is a grey area that scientists and herbalists could collaborate, but they haven't been able to find a meeting point. Mostly due to pride and arrogance, which I myself personally witnessed. It is sad that the two sections of society do not integrate well, as I believe both could help each other to make several lifesaving advances simply by studying nature and using medicine to replicate it in a way that is not harmful or damaging to the human body.

Please remember that I had leukaemia. Most herbalist studies are founded on the fact that you can heal yourself by the foods you put into your system. These foods while carrying nutrients, attack the cancerous cells, often making tumours, lumps and bumps and even certain mental diseases to dissolve over a matter of time. The basic underlying belief is that if you can make your body alkaline, then your body will naturally start to attack any cancerous cell as they tend to grow in acidic environments. OK? Good. Well then let me ask you… What about when you have a blood disease, and your blood cannot carry the nutrients in the first place?

I personally didn't have any lumps or bumps; I had a blood disorder. This soon became an issue for me, because no matter how much kale and apricot juices I had or moringa and turmeric tablets I took, my cancer still managed to get worse. The evidence of which was apparent in my fingers, as that was the first initial sign of me having cancer. Remember? My hand was swollen initially; this was due to a leukemic cell build up. This then meant any medicine that was introduced would first have to combat that issue. The reason for this wasn't complicated. My blood simply couldn't carry the nutrients, and therefore my body was not benefiting from my new diet. Let me; please reiterate, I FULLY BELIEVE in herbal remedies if anyone has anything non-blood related.

Moving on...

So, after giving the herbal route a try for a month, I decided to take the hospital route and after two weeks of chemo, I had my hand back in its natural form. Great, right? Until they tell you all the stuff you may have to deal with as a result of the treatment. At which point you then have to weigh up what you want out of life and move forward. Honestly, western medicine saved my life, because herbal practices weren't practical to my situation. I believe that anyone who does get ill should always try to do the herbalist (organic) route first and if it doesn't pan out the way in which is beneficial to your life, then go ahead with the western medicine.

Chapter 8: The Flip Side

This section is crucial to me because it highlights the significance of not letting a situation get the best of you. Admittedly, I went through a lot yet I was able to survive and beat cancer twice over the space of two years whilst graduating with a 2:1 and a Dean's Award whilst simultaneously running a network marketing business from hospital. The struggle of having cancer is what allowed me to get my Dean's Award. In reality, had I not gone above and beyond whilst in the hospital, I never would have got it and therefore wouldn't be able to share this achievement with you. If I never had cancer I would never have had something to overcome, nor would I have been celebrated for overcoming it. Do you see my point?

Struggling in general sucks, however, if you never had to struggle you can never help someone else to become better because you yourself have no prior experience of what it means to come against an adverse situation and win. The reason I'm saying all this is simple. Throughout my journey, my struggle, the thing that was meant to kill me has allowed me to meet some incredible people. I had the pleasure of meeting Sir Richard Branson (founder of Virgin), and through that experience, I was also able to meet a lovely lady called Lynne, who was in charge of Richard's PR. Lynne, till today has consistently checked up on me via email, from my first year of cancer until recently, even after me being given the all clear. She still greats me with the same warm enthusiasm that she always did even though her initial job was facilitating the meeting between me and Richard Branson and even now that the meeting is over and been over for a while now. Such kind people, I would never have met if it weren't for my struggle. Now please understand I am not trying to boast in the fact that I met Richard Branson. My reasoning is simple, had I not been ill, I would probably never have met the man. I'm not saying get ill so that you can meet people! Rather the fact, that there are some things in life you just cannot control, but you can control how you act in those situations, and you can also manage the relationships you build in those situations.

Another example of this, again by no real effort on my part was the fact that I was published in a newspaper. Why? Because of the fact I graduated with cancer. This allowed me to meet Marcia who owns an online Blog/ Magazine, which has 1000s of subscribers. She did a whole article on my achievement, congratulating me the whole time because of the struggle that I had been through. This, in turn, allowed me to meet a gentleman by the name of Yinka, who works for Premier Gospel Radio, who then invited me to be on the show to also share my story. Both these incredible people allowed me to share my story with thousands of people. They both blessed me incredibly, so much so, I don't know how I would pay them back. The point I'm trying to make is very simple.

No struggle, No story
No Test, No Testimony
No Battle fought, No Medal given

It might sound pretty obvious but think about your own life for a second. What's happening that is negative in your life right now? What can you do, speak to, be around? That will allow you to turn this negative situation into a positive for the future. Or even better, what can you personally learn! From this situation that will make you better? An example could be you had a financial problem, that got way out of control, that you then were able to resolve in a way, which most people don't/ can't. You now have a lesson that can be shared to influence the lives of those around you. Yes, it was painful, you had bills, you lost sleep, you argued with your spouse, etc., but you overcame. You now have something that a lot of people in the world need to know because people who have yet to go through your experience can use what you have already been through to combat life rather than to be attacked by it.

So what now? In the grand scheme of things, these are just a few of the lessons that I learned while in hospital. Later on ill have a bigger book that covers all the little stories in between that helped me get to this place that I am currently at right now regarding mindset and positivity, but these were a few of the major ones.

I wanted to share these with you, because it took me to get cancer TWICE, to understand a lot more about what is important in life. In short, its relationship and legacy.

Honestly, the thing of most importance now that I can walk, I have all my bodily functions back and I'm cancer free is building my relationships and friendships. There is not one person I take for granted in this life and I'm always trying my best to work on them and let people know I care about them. The relationships you build with people on a daily basis and your legacy (the way in which you conduct yourself daily in all the things that you do), allow you to leave this world with an imprint that states, no matter what this world threw at me, this is how I dealt with it. One thing my dad taught me, at a very young age was the power of books and shared information.

"If am man lives for 50 years and dies but he wrote all the lessons that life had taught him in a book and handed it down to you, and you read that book in a month, that then means you have managed to acquire 50 years of knowledge in a month!"

Is that not incredible?! If that's the case, please read, so that you can gain wisdom and learn the lessons of those that came before you, so you yourself don't make the same mistake. That is the purpose of this book, so that you don't need to wait till you've had an experience like mine to not only know about these principles, but to also APPLY THEM to your life, or at least try to.

Due to my own experiences that I have stated I am now striving to be a motivational speaker. Having spoken at conferences and on the radio, my aim is now to make people deeply look at themselves and show them the strength that they each possess. With that being said, I hope you learned something.

"Love, Live, bless and be blessed by the overcoming of fear and by the acceptance of Joy and faith."

Kierran Jarrett –
Author| Inspirational Speaker and Mentor

21073936R00034

Printed in Poland
by Amazon Fulfillment
Poland Sp. z o.o., Wrocław